DOGS

Their True Origin, Function, and Future

A Study in Spiritual Unfolding

DOGS

Their True Origin, Function, and Future

ALEKSANDRA MIKIC

PORTAL BOOKS
2013

2013
PORTAL BOOKS
128 Second Place, Brooklyn, New York 11231

LIBRARY OF CONGRESS CATALOGING-IN-PUBLICATION DATA
is available on request.

Print ISBN : 978-1-938685-06-4
eBook ISBN : 978-1-938685-07-1

Contents

Introduction

The intertwined journey of human and dog has spurred the interests of anthropologists, biologists, historians, sociologists, and behavioral scientists. After all, the dog is "man's best friend," so it is natural that people have wondered about how, why, from where, and when dogs came to be.

The "from where" part seemed simple enough to answer—one just needed to look at the dog's wild brother, and with Darwin's blessing conclude that the dog's origin is the wolf. The rest of the questions have proved to be more difficult to answer. Is it because the original assumption led people astray? That is one of the questions I hope to answer in this book: is the dog just a domesticated wolf?

If it is not, how can we explain the extraordinary similarity—for example, sixty-three days of gestation, nearly identical DNA, and interbreeding that produces viable offspring? If these things are true, why are dogs and wolves so fundamentally different? Consider the wolf's stable form versus the plasticity of the dog's, their different timing of sexual maturity, that the wolf gives birth once a year and the dog twice, that the wolf shies away from humans while the dog seeks them out. If they are not the same, then what is the dog's true origin? If they are the same, why do humans traditionally hate the wolf and consider the dog their best friend? If these questions, and others that will arise in the process of inquiry, are truthfully answered, then all of the scientific disciplines could be applied without conflict, which is certainly not the case today.

1

Taming the Beast

Once the dog was termed "domesticated wolf," different theories popped up to explain just how and when this domestication took place. Scientists definitely do not agree on when—some say 12,000 years ago, some say 150,000 years ago, others say 400,000 years ago. The method they use to determine the timing remains unclear because to this day from human sites there has been no archaeological evidence uncovered of any transition from wolves to dogs.

The most accepted theory of domestication is that prehistoric humans collected wolf pups, kept and tamed them, and over many generations wolves became domestic dogs. This theory has more holes in it than Swiss cheese, but respected people have claimed it on national television. They say the reason prehistoric humans would collect wolf pups in the first place was their desire to have a pet. How the concept of a pet would arise in the prehistoric mind is anyone's guess.

Let us, for just a moment, assume that this is true. We have to ask why a wolf would be chosen and not something less dangerous, like a rat? How would these wolves be stopped from running away when their hormones surged? And here comes the "deal breaker" question: Would they give birth to tame offspring?

The difference between tame and domestic has to be discussed here. Tame just means friendly. Many individual wild animals can be tamed to some degree, but domestic really means giving birth to tame offspring. Dog pups are born tame, they can be socialized late in their development and they naturally seek human contact. Assuming good health (without rabies, brain tumor, or other diseases), a dog would have to be treated harshly to avoid humans.

So dogs are domestic, but not every individual dog is necessarily tame, and we can see plenty of those parading through Cesar Millan's *Dog Whisperer* television episodes. Wolf pups, on the other hand, are born wild. To be tame enough to accept human contact, they have to be handled before their eyes open and heavily socialized before they are three weeks old. Anything later than that fails every time.

This sounds like a lot of work for our prehistoric friends. What would be their reward, considering a high risk of being bitten, killed, bleeding to death, etc.? Could they train a wolf to do their bidding? Anyone who has given a command to a wolf knows that one might give the same command to a chair with the same result—neither responds.

We can now safely walk away from this theory, and we would certainly not be the first to do so. Realizing that taming individual wild wolves can never result in a domestic population of dogs, some scientists explored other venues. Since wolves and humans have a similar social structure and both are hunters, maybe there would be mutual benefit if they joined forces?

Here is a quote from Lee Charles Kelly, a dog trainer, that illustrates this theory: "We may have very well let the wolves do the killing and even let them have the organ meat, we just wanted to scavenge that fresh, juicy muscle tissue."[1]

If Mr. Kelly had come across the writings of Weston A. Price, he would have known that both humans and wolves competed for the organs and couldn't care less for the muscle tissue. Price described a North American tribe that commonly harvested organs from a moose and threw the muscle tissue to the dogs.

Some went as far as to say that wolves domesticated us. Others gave up entirely on explanation and said that even though we don't know how the process of domestication happened, it did happen, so there you go.

The event that seemed to cement in the fact of domestication was Dmitry Belyaev's experiment with silver foxes on a fur farm in Russia in the 1950s. The intention was to create tame foxes that could be easily handled on the farm by selecting animals based on their flight distance.

However, along with acquiring tameness, the foxes started changing their form and looking a whole lot like dogs (with floppy ears, spotted fur, shorter legs) and so finally there was living proof of how wolves became dogs. Or was there?

If we want to be really scientific, we have to admit that the only thing this experiment proved is that foxes change form under human pressure of domestication through selective breeding. The same happens with pigs, but as soon as they are set free, within a couple of generations the wild form returns. These foxes were not let loose, so nobody knows what would have happened to them. And while no pressure is applied to feral dogs, they never start to resemble wolves.

What about wolf breeding programs? They do exist, but no change of form ever took place, nor did they ever give birth to tame offspring. Just how stable is the wolf form? We don't need to search further than the wolf-dog hybrids. The only official/scientific way to determine whether an animal is a hybrid is by the way it looks! There is no blood or DNA test, or anything else that can determine the presence of wolf blood, just the form.

It doesn't even matter how small the percentage of wolf blood there is since these animals always resemble wolves in both behavior and form. So the short answer is that the wolf form is superbly stable; we can't change it even when we try. To us, this will be very important because form is the library of the organism, if one can read it.

Biologist Raymond Coppinger traveled the world in search of original feral populations of dogs. He correctly observed that wolves and dogs represent different species and that original feral dogs have a similar form no matter where in the world they are found: color is either uniform or patchy, mostly yellow, weight is about thirty pounds, the ears floppy, and their nature low-key and friendly. They are equally likely to form small groups as to live a solitary existence. Bahamian dogs, called "potcakes," fit this description perfectly. The point is that they are dogs and not some half-species between wolves and dogs.

After forty-five years of raising, training, and studying the behavior of dogs worldwide, Coppinger and his wife, biologist Lorna Coppinger, in spite of their observations, conclude that evolution of form still took place; however, they place it with the entire populations as opposed to the individual animals. They write: "The wild wolf, *Canis lupus*, began to separate into populations that could make a living at the dumps and those that couldn't. Within one segment of the population, the frequency increased of those genes that resulted in tamer wolves, and that population could be said to have been evolving toward a new species."[2]

It was Belyaev's fox experiment that inspired the Coppingers' theory of evolution. The idea is that the animals with the least flight distance benefited the most from human dump sites and therefore had the greatest opportunity to procreate. Of course, in Belyaev's experiments, human pressure was applied in terms of selective breeding, while in nature there is nobody to put pressure on the wolves.

This theory echoes Darwin's theory of natural selection, which claims that the survival of the species is dependent on the specific adaptation to the environment. Therefore the evolutionary direction would lead toward greater and greater dependence on the environment. Let's see what nature has to say for herself in terms of the development of species.

The obvious difference between any plant and any animal, even the simple amoeba, is movement. A single-celled organism has the power of locomotion and a sensory system that allows it to move toward pleasure and away from pain. Plants can't uproot and leave; they are open to whatever their environment dishes out to them. If there is no food in the soil, they wither and die. They cannot change location. It seems that, even from the start, the animal kingdom has more freedom and less dependence on the environment than the plants do. We can say that even the simplest of animals have freed their membrane, or their outer cover, from direct dependence on the environment.

The class of invertebrates (animals without a spinal column, such as insects and worms) has a sensory system that functions independently from the environment, but there is no enclosed nervous system to speak of. The next on the evolutionary ladder are the animals with a central nerve cord. In fish, the frontal part of the cord becomes the brain. The first vertebrates have therefore emancipated the nervous system in addition to the sensory system.

Fish breathe through their gills, organs on the outside of the body, but amphibians enclose their breathing system by developing lungs. They remain totally dependent on the environment for moisture—their fluid system stays open. It will be emancipated by the reptiles that develop the heart and closed-off circulation.

Reptiles remain temperature dependent on their environment, however. You probably know that reptiles become lethargic and slow when it's cold outside, and quick and more aggressive when it's hot. Their entire metabolism shifts with the change in weather. Birds succeed in freeing the temperature control. By being able to maintain constant body temperature, they free their internal organs from the influence of the environment.

Up to this point in evolution, almost all bodily systems become independent, but there is still the question of reproduction. The young embryos are at the mercy of the environment, developing in eggs outside of mother's body. They are exposed to predators, weather changes, and all the other factors that arise in the environment. Birds at least protect their eggs and keep them warm, but sea turtles, for example, bury them in the sand and leave them to their fate.

And then come the mammals that liberate the reproductive system from the influence of the environment. Now the offspring is developing in the uterus, inside the mother's body, staying safe and protected as long as she is. Upon their birth, the young ones do not have to seek food, as mother's milk nourishes them while they grow.

The more the animal kingdom differentiates, the more independent of the environment it becomes. This observable truth stands in direct opposition to the theory of natural selection and adaptation to the environment. The order in which the organ systems become emancipated is from the head downward, in the direction of the descent of the spirit.

Darwin's theory of natural selection took the meaning out of evolution. Up to that time, the word "evolution" meant the life lifting itself up from below, or developing further, and it carried an idea of greater purpose. With Darwin's theory, the striving toward a goal was erased and became nothing more than competition. To understand how that idea came about, we should look at the society, culture, and science of the time.

Every time period has its particular social, cultural, historical, scientific, and economic complex, which is interlaced, and the idea that appears in one part of the complex easily permeates the rest. The previous idea of what evolution meant was manifesting itself in social unrest and revolutions, but then industrial capitalism was born.

Suddenly, there was the economic market competition, which seemed to be part luck and part business sense. Such profound change in social structure echoed in all other areas, including history and biology, and resulted in the idea of biological competition, or natural selection.

So you see, Darwin's thinking was inextricably intertwined with other impactful things of his time. With the focus shifting toward economy, competition, quantities, and numbers, science became entirely permeated by it as well. Note the economy-like language in the quote below.

> Owing to this struggle for life, any variation, however slight and from whatever cause proceeding, if it be in any degree profitable to an individual of any species, in its infinitely complex relations to other organic beings and to external nature, will tend to the preservation of that individual, and will generally be inherited by its offspring.[3]

As the human being is considered the grand finale of evolution, what can we learn from our own nature and our relationship with the environment?

As spirit makes its full descent into human beings, we should expect to find even greater emancipation from the environment, and we do. While animals are extremely well suited to particular environments, they are not able to survive in others. We can't imagine horses living in trees, squirrels in the ocean, or birds underground. Yet, human beings live all over the earth; we can live in tree houses, earth homes, and igloos. We can also fly in the air in airplanes and sink to the bottom of the ocean in submarines.

Human beings have freed their limb system. Compared with animals, our limbs are unspecialized, while animal limbs are tools in and of themselves. Birds have wings that take them into the air, horses have hooves to pound across open plains, ocean animals have fins to move through the water, squirrels have claws to climb trees, and so on. Animals are born with tools, and humans have to make their own. The more that an animal is specialized for one environment, the more it is bound to it.

From all of the above, we can see that there is a definite order in the development of the species, and that order is the result of an evolutionary impulse. That impulse is the emancipation from the environment, or freedom. It is the polar opposite from Darwin's notion.

Regardless of the explanation they state, all the theories regarding the evolution of form fall apart in the same moment—the present. Surely someone, somewhere, would have seen a wolf mother with at least one doggish-looking pup, or wolf packs hanging around human dump sites. Bears, however, do hang around! Maybe they should be the ones evolving into pets. Joking aside, there is no evidence of any half-species existing today, or of any co-operation between wolves and humans. The conclusion is clear — the dog is not a tame wolf, and no process of domestication could ever have influenced the wolf's unchanging form.

If evolution according to Darwin did not happen, what did? How did dogs appear in this world? Let's expand that question and ask about all of the species and kingdoms of nature.

2

The True Origin of Species

Seeing things in a way we haven't seen them before is similar to taking up a new sport. At first we are awkward and clumsy, and use a greater number of muscles than we need to. If we stick with it, the muscles become more efficient, flexible, and strong, and the whole activity more effortless.

In the case that follows, we will be developing some supersensible muscles. We need to think in a holistic way, with our whole mind. The first rule of holistic thinking is the acceptance of supersensible reality. It is safe to assume that you love dogs—why else would you be reading this book? That love of yours can't be seen, touched, smelled, tasted, or heard and yet it's real. You are already on your way!

Rules of Holistic Thinking

Acceptance of supersensible reality

Our sensory organs continuously stream in the evidence of the material world. The challenge is to develop the organs of supersensible perception that reveal the meaning of that world. The consciousness that receives the data determines the understanding.

The scientist who ushered the way of true observation of nature was Johann Wolfgang von Goethe (1749-1832). If you look him up in an encyclopedia, it is likely that the word "scientist" is not next to his name. This is a consequence of the loss of our capacity to behold nature as it truly is, today's reduction of science to quantitative measurements, and the separation between subject and object.

But like hound dogs, we will follow the trail of the dynamic thinkers who grasped and expanded the way Goethe saw nature, and acquire that capacity for ourselves. We must always strive to see beyond appearances, beyond symptoms, beyond the dots, and into the inclusive depth of phenomena. When you look at a painting made up of dots, it takes you a little time before the intended image bursts into your mind. The sensory input remains the same, but your processing of it shifts. Supersensible organs are about connecting the dots. Think of all the times when you said, "I see" in response to an explanation. What were you seeing with? And how?

You were seeing with your imagination. Imagination is the active aspect of the mind that sees and grasps a meaning simultaneously and is capable of building connections. The mind is not a mirror, simply reflecting what the senses perceive. Through its imagining capacity interacting with the sensory imprint, it gives rise to the phenomena—the supersensible reality—the world of meaning.

We must not think of meaning as an object that the mind attaches to reality, because the imagination experiences phenomena directly; it does not perceive any separation between subject and object. The perception of meaning is not the result of the senses grasping one extra thing. Rather it is the result of the shift in seeing from sensory to imaginary without wiping out the sensory.

For example, here are some black lines on a white background, shaped like this: DOG. What did your imagination see? The lines are still there, and they convey a meaning that is also there. You are seeing both, aren't you?

When you were first learning to speak, you didn't have a concept of what a dog was until the word "dog" lit up that concept in your mind. When we are learning a second language, we already have the concepts, and we assign different names to them, so we assume that is how we have learned the first language as well — that we had concepts and needed names for them. But, really, nothing could be further from the truth. It was the language that caused the world of phenomena to appear for us. Therefore, the word and the phenomenon are inextricably linked, and "DOG" will never be just black lines on a white background.

Mechanism vs. wholism

There is a serious disease sweeping people's minds, which we can call "particle-ism." We have become so enamored with the concepts of matter, machines, mechanics, and parts, that they pervade our thinking even when it comes to living organisms. The dive into physical matter is searching for the ever-smaller particles, just as doctors are specializing in just one human part. We are taught that the cells are the building blocks of life. How did we ever land in Legoland?

In the mechanistic view, parts build up the whole. In the holistic view, the whole differentiates into parts. The difference is profound, as the whole preceding the parts presumes a living intelligence guiding the process, developing the idea, multiplying itself.

To understand these concepts better, let's compare the puzzle with a hologram. Puzzle pieces are true parts that build up the whole picture, and it is not possible to discern the whole from just one, or even a few. The hologram always reflects the whole, even in the broken parts. Therefore, even the parts are whole. Our goal is to use this holographic idea to discern the supersensible reality. In other words, we will engage bigger holograms, which are truly the organizing ideas and which can only be seen with the mind.

Imagine an exhibition in a museum you know nothing about beforehand, and the first exhibit you see is a painting of a young girl's face. The next one is a close up photograph of an old man with the sun shining on his face in such a way that every wrinkle and crease shows clearly. Then you come upon a bronze bust of a famous poet. And then you realize that they are all portraits, and that is the theme of the exhibition, or the hologram you've been looking for. All the exhibits are not broken parts of some giant portrait that you can see with your eyes, but you do see it with your mind. Each piece of the exhibit is whole in its own right, and yet reflects the greater whole. So is each living organism an embodiment of a spiritual idea, perfect and whole.

Now we are ready to embark on the revelatory journey and discover the origin of the kingdoms of nature. We will see that all of them are holographic aspects of an underlying evolutionary process.

Fourfold Organization

The fourfold organization is well known in the spiritual science of anthroposophy. What follows is a crash course. We can't stray too far from our focus on the species of dog, and yet we must have a basic understanding of what evolution really is. For deeper exploration of this subject, you are encouraged to read the books listed in the resources section. This chapter is truly a very small summary of what they provide in much greater depth.

It is now time to apply the rules of holistic thinking we just learned. I told you it was a crash course! Let's connect the dots and show a direct resonance between:

- four gestures of embryonic development,
- four supersensible bodies of the organism (physical, etheric, astral, ontic),
- four kingdoms of nature (mineral, plant, animal, human),
- four elements (earth, water, air, fire), and
- four stages of creation.

Embryonic development is a very special gift of revelation, because it reflects the truth of all other evolutionary and living processes. It is like a fast-forward version of developments that otherwise take years, centuries, or eons and would therefore escape our perceptual grasp. Embryonic development recapitulates the unfolding of the earth, of the species, and even of the individual life that is to come.

The mineral realm

The physical body and the mineral kingdom seem so material, don't they? You may wonder if a mineral even has a supersensible reality. It certainly does. On the one hand, it is the manifestation of a spiritual impulse, birthed by a spiritual entity; but the spiritual entity that brought it forth does not reside within it. On the other hand, "the body" doesn't necessarily reflect just the body we can touch, but anything that is accrued, such as a body of law, a body of evidence, a scientific body, and so on.

This brings us to the very essence that defines the physical, the earth, and the mineral nature, namely the adding on, the repetition, the accruing of the same element. Think about the growth of a crystal—maybe you have done it as a science project. The same substance keeps on growing by adding on more of the same. There is no inside and outside, no life, no movement, just adding on.

If you were to cut a rock or a crystal, you would reveal another outside surface, and you would have two rocks instead of one. The cut off part doesn't have any function that differs from the whole. Compare that to cutting a tree or the limb of a living being. That is very different, isn't it?

A mineral is pure form, fully finished from the start, and it is timeless. There are no stages of development that a rock needs to go through the way living beings do. Minerals can change, but such change is brought upon them by outside forces such as water erosion, for example, and it is never initiated from within. Minerals fill the space without any predetermined shape. They have only a physical body, and are therefore fully subject to the laws of matter, such as Newtonian physics. Our physical body is our mineral nature internalized, while mineral earth is our mineral nature externalized.

The first week of embryonic development reflects the mineral nature—there is a division without any differentiation. Note that it is the division within the whole, and not a simple adding on of parts. The embryo is the constant reminder that wholeness is the mark of life, and that it is always there first before the parts come into being. This stage lasts one week in all mammals regardless of the length of gestation. This shows us that time is not yet relevant but will be ushered in with the arrival of the plant nature.

The plant realm

The plant kingdom embodies life, and it directly opposes gravity. We have all seen a blade of grass push right through concrete. Mechanical laws no longer apply. The plant grows and metamorphoses, as opposed to just adding on the same elements the way minerals do. There is the appearance of definite shape and of metabolism through which the plant interacts with the outside world.

The organs of the plant appear in sequential order— and time, as one marker of life, has entered the picture. The gesture we see is one of reaching outward toward the periphery. When a video is made of a plant growing from a seed, and then played in fast motion, that outward reach becomes obvious. The whole plant is open to the outside and completely exposed. In fact, there is no real inside content to speak of. All the plant's organs are seen on the outside, with none hidden within — and being underground doesn't qualify as within!

Animals and humans also have a plant nature; this is called the etheric body. Its other names — time body, life body, formative body — all represent the attributes of the etheric body externalized in plants. The element associated with the ether body is water, frequently called the element that brings life. When the element of water interacts with the element of earth, form arises; clay can be shaped when it is softened with water.

The ether body is vitality, regeneration, and life. It is the building up, shaping, radial force. Think about how resistant to entropy living beings are, how faithful the organism is to its form, healing wounds and scars, knitting broken bones, always trying to return to its original template. This intelligence, the force that keeps our form, is our etheric body, which descends upon the embryo in the second week of development.

The second week is the implantation stage, when the embryo radically changes its organizing principle to become plant-like, rooting itself into the maternal tissue. Another mark of life is polarity, which now shows itself in the opposing tendencies. The trophoblast is reaching outward, while the embryoblast holds back. Extending toward the periphery is the dominant gesture, and the tro-phoblast is actively absorbing nutrition from the mother. The tension grows between the opposing tendencies within the embryo, and threatens to either rip it apart or grow a plant-like animal or human.

The animal realm

The animal is an ensouled being that moves and breathes, completely opposite from the plant, which is stationary and only exchanges gases. Many traditional cultures speak of breath and soul interchangeably. The organs that are visible on the outside of the plant are within the animal. They do not succeed each other through metamorphosis but are there from the beginning, growing and changing through time.

While plants eventually die, death is truly the mark of the animal, representing the final moment when the force of catabolism overcomes life. We can now speak of the pre-determined life cycle and the programmed cell death. When cells are grown in vitro, healthy animal cells die after a certain number of divisions, but plant and cancer cells do not.

Animals have surrendered some of their vitality to the forces of breaking down, in exchange for being conscious. The forces of regeneration are inversely proportionate to the level of consciousness, therefore the lower animals are able to regenerate their limbs. In them, the plant nature is still quite dominant.

Animal growth is focused inward, opposite from the outward striving of the plant. The pleasure principle enters the picture, as the animal knows what it wants and actively seeks it. The soul is said to descend from the stars and is therefore called the astral body, associated with the element of air. Note that air is the only element that can be compressed and expanded, just like the breath.

The astral body penetrates the etheric/physical complex through the nervous system, and brings with it not just pleasure but also pain. The balance between the astral and etheric/physical complex becomes crucial. The sheer dominance of the astral would culminate in a frozen form, while the sheer dominance of the etheric/physical complex would end in chaos and dissolution.

We have left the story of the embryo at a very critical juncture: as it is about to be torn apart by the opposing forces of its plant stage, unless a new principle comes to the rescue. That new principle is the descent of the soul.

Animals are conscious, and with consciousness a new differentiation comes into play. Plants do not differentiate in the level of vitality they possess in terms of different species. We can say that one tomato plant is more vital than another, but we cannot say that the species of tomato is more vital than the species of pepper. Animals, however, differ greatly in their level of consciousness.

Consciousness is an animal quality, not present in plants, and therefore has nothing to do with arising out of complexity, as Darwin's notion would have it. The most complex plants are not conscious, while the most primitive animals are. This shows us that consciousness incarnates, and it does so in the embryo around the seventeenth day.

> These three, the ego, the astral body and the ether body, are those which then descend on the seventeenth day. But by that day the development must be such that a house is prepared for the three, so that they may move in.

> — Dr. Karl König, *Embryology and World Evolution* [4]

In the physical realm, at this moment in the life of the embryo, the mesoderm appears, and with it a third dimension, the true inner content. The mesoderm connects the two opposing poles and creates space for the soul to incarnate. It is the origin of blood.

At first, the blood starts flowing from the periphery to the center of the embryo. Once there it stops, as there is nowhere to go, and then reverses direction. In this space, where the direction of the circulation reverses and where the rhythm exists, the heart manifests. So you see, circulation precedes the heart. The heart is not a pump, because a pump is not needed. The origin of circulation never changes throughout life—it is always in the capillaries, at the periphery of the organism. The heart has a more noble function as the organ of the incarnation of the soul.

We have seen so far that there are no gradual changes for the embryo. It is more like an "all or nothing" proposition. Each time, a complete change of the functioning paradigm is required, and many embryos do not make it through these moments of crisis. With the understanding that the embryo recapitulates the evolution of the four kingdoms of nature, and that includes the individual species, we begin to realize that gradual evolution really never happened.

The human realm

So far, we have determined that minerals have matter; that plants have matter and life; and that animals have matter, life, and soul. Each kingdom gives up something of itself for the next one to emerge. No kingdom is the extension of the previous one, rather they stand in opposition. And the same is true for the individual animal organism, where the etheric body overcomes the laws of matter, and the astral body sets boundaries on life and growth.

It follows that the human realm must oppose animal nature in some way and surrender some of its gifts. What does the animal have that the human no longer does? Powerful instincts, for one thing; physical prowess for another. And what has taken control of the astral body and allowed a human being to transcend animal nature? It is the descent of the spirit.

There comes a time in each young child's life when he or she starts to use the word "I." Self-reflection is the mark of the spirit.

> Man is psychically distinguished from all other animals by the entirely new fact that he not only knows, but knows that he knows.
>
> — Pierre Teilhard de Chardin, *The Phenomenon of Man* [5]

The more we interact with animals, the more their individual spirit awakens. We see the examples of animals using sign language, recognizing themselves in the mirror, acting in ways opposing their survival instincts. Yet, we understand that individual responsibility does not rest with them. The animal can kill, but not murder. It is not responsible for its actions (but its owner is).

The "I" or the spirit is associated with the element of fire, the only element that can permeate all others, reflecting the supremacy of the spirit. Things appear and disappear in fire, showing us that fire is an element of manifestation and transformation.

What gesture does the embryo offer to mark the descent of spirit? In the early stages of development, all embryos are human-like. But then there comes a moment when the embryo stretches out, corresponding to standing up.

Human embryos maintain this gesture, while animal embryos never stretch out completely. Subsequently, animals do not resist the pull of gravity, and always succumb to it in some way.

The way a human being stands is very different from way other bipeds stand. Our center of gravity is positioned in such a way that standing upright is based on balancing and does not require effort. In addition, our upper part, arms, hands, and the head, move independently and are not necessary for locomotion. Therefore, only a human being achieves the full tension between the earth and the spirit pole, and is able to effortlessly maintain it, just as the human embryo achieves the full stretch and maintains it.

Through the organism of warmth and the element of fire, the "I" or the spirit permeates all the other bodies and becomes the primary guiding force. While animals are primarily guided by their feelings, humans must be guided by the individual spirit.

The individual spirit gives the astral body its purpose and unique personality. It gives the etheric body the individual memory and the physical body individual shape. It is due to our spirit that we are aware of our past and that we can anticipate the future—which seems to be both a gift and a curse. Just think about how many books have been written teaching us how to live in the now! Animals, on the other hand, can *only* live in the now, and it is we humans who keep the memory of the continuity of their lives.

The Whole That Preceded the Parts

We have already pointed out that the parts do not build up the whole, but that the whole is there first, differentiating itself into parts. In the case of the natural world, there is obviously no physical whole of any kind. But there is an idea, a paradigm that came into being in response to the impulse of freedom, which then unfolded itself in an organized way.

We can liken it to a composer who has an impulse to write music, and he puts his idea down on the manuscript sheet. The idea unfolds itself as an orchestra plays that music from the beginning to the end. While the ending note seems like a culmination of the piece, it is just an unfolding of an idea that was already there, written down on the sheet.

Once again, we will return to the embryo and its story of recapitulation. If one idea stands before all the species, then all the embryos must have something in common that would show itself in the beginning of the soul phase of development, right before they differentiate into different species. We have mentioned it already; they are all human-like.

It is the idea of the human that unfolds itself, guided by the impulse of achieving freedom. As this idea unfolded, it branched out into many different species, each representing an inner aspect of the human brought to perfection. It is correct to say that the idea of the human is the ancestor of all animal species, and of the natural world as a whole.

> The esotericist says: "Everything in the surrounding world—stones, plants and animals—are signposts along the path of my own evolution. Without these kingdoms I could not exist.
>
> — Rudolf Steiner, *Foundations of Esotericism* [6]

Animals are in no way a failed attempt at creating a human; rather each is the end result of an impulse that has been released into perfection. The human being has retained its imperfection in exchange for the descent of the individual spirit; with it, it has received freedom and responsibility.

In *The Wholeness of Nature*, Henri Bortoft writes that truth is neither singular nor plural, but multiple. Therefore, humans and animals are one multiple archetypal organism unfolding itself. This is no different in principle than the archetypal plant seen by Goethe.

Humans must hold tension, not allowing any inner aspect to precipitate within themselves and escape control of the spirit. Our inner aspects precipitate outward in the kingdoms that surround us. We can compare humans and animals to the seed and petals of a flower. The seed contains the potential of the flower, but where would the beauty be without the petals unfolding?

Evolution vs. Creation

We can now see the futility of the opposition between creationists and Darwinists, as neither sees the greater truth. If they did, they could experience the beauty and logic of the truth that is grander than they are currently imagining. Creationists understand that there is a divine power behind this world, but they see it as frozen, denying the unfolding aspect. Darwinists deny the spiritual impulse and therefore cannot properly understand the unfolding.

The belief in completed forms giving rise to other forms is unsupportable not just by science but by common sense. Any living organism that varies too much from its original template self-destructs; it does not miraculously morph into some other form. There is no evidence whatsoever of any half-forms being discovered. In other words, there are no in-between species.

The clincher would be the simple question of where they are today. If species are always adapting, who can point out a single change that has been verified in a species as a whole? Instead, the tendency is to think of evolution as something that has happened in the past and is standing still now. Who decides when the species stops evolving and when? The only evolution going on is the evolution of consciousness, where each thrust of the spirit results in a different inner world and precipitates itself in the outer.

The species are not the procession of forms connected through procreation. Rather, they are the progression of one organism expressing itself. This organism is dynamic, manifesting as complete forms without ever completing itself. When this organism is grasped through the imaginary capacity, it is like the dawning of language. It is suddenly lit up inside you, and you cannot "un-see" it. Scripture tells us that in the beginning there was the word!

We have to see the simultaneous descent of spirit and the heightening of nature as two poles of one process. Driven by the impulse for freedom, the spirit and earth beings unite to birth the natural world through love. Due to the holographic nature of the world, every time two beings unite in love, they are recapitulating this original idea. Spirit must fully descend for nature to fully ascend and express the original paradigm—the idea of Humanity.

It is worth repeating that the only evolution going on is the evolution of consciousness and of ever-greater love between spirit and earth. The two unite in a myriad of ways, as many as there are species in this world. Each species and each organism is a unique expression of that love. The way these forces interpenetrate within the organism is revealed in its threefold organization—the living form.

3

The Living Form

Goethe's famous statement, "The lion has no horns and cannot have any" ushered in a new kind of biology, the biology of meaning. There is no aspect of spatial or temporal form that is accidental—nature is imbued with intelligent order. Through their forms, animals speak to us of the processes that govern their being; of their resonance with certain aspects of Humanity; of their function, origin, and purpose.[7]

To truly understand the being of Dog, we have to understand the forces that shape it through time and space. Rudolf Steiner has revealed to us that humanity is the model according to which the wholeness of nature can be understood, and that the appearance of the species is the outer manifestation of an inner process. The entire natural world is a giant organism reflecting humanity's inner world, and we can discover the precise resonance between the species and the organic process in both time and space.

No one has taken Goethe's understanding of animal form to greater depths than Wolfgang Schad. He has fully unraveled the code of the threefold organization of the external organism we call the natural world. To understand where "man's best friend" belongs, we have to see the whole picture and the dominant typologies within.

> The threefold approach seeks to derive the living organism from nothing but itself. Such objective observation reveals an ordered diversity that always permits antagonistic opposites to exist within it. Moreover, this universal order requires balancing, mediating, regulating functions to exist, in which the opposites come together. Polarities and their active mediation are the fundamental processes that constitute every living organism. Threefoldness is therefore one of the universal signs of life.[8]

The three distinct functional systems are the nerve-sense system (thinking), the respiratory-circulatory or rhythmic system (feeling), and the metabolic-limb system (will). The head is the center of the thinking system, the chest is the center of the feeling system, and the lower abdomen is the center of the will.

> It is of utmost importance to see clearly the relationship between the function of the nerves, the breathing system, and the activity of the metabolism. These three forms of activity do not lie beside one another but in one another. They permeate and pass over into one another.
>
> — Rudolf Steiner, *Riddles of the Soul* [9]

40

While each system has its respective center, its processes are always found throughout the organism. Each organism is formed space and formed time. Looking at a human body, we see bilateral symmetry. This applies especially to the sensory organs; therefore symmetry is the formative principle of the system, which is open to the outside world. The organs of metabolism, on the other hand, are closed off from the outside world and take up space in a very different way. They are asymmetrical in their individual form as well as in their position toward the body's axis of symmetry.

While in humans the threefold organization is perfectly balanced, in the animal world we find the emphasis of one process over the others, which is the reason behind the specialization of form. It is important that the division

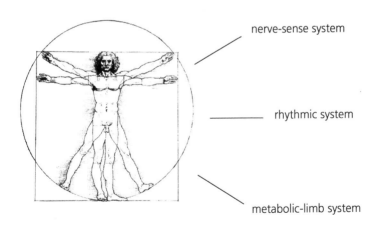

nerve-sense system

rhythmic system

metabolic-limb system

that follows is not viewed in a linear way, but that we keep in mind thorough interpenetration of the nerve-sense, metabolic-limb, and rhythmic processes.

Among mammals, the animal that best represents the dominance of the nerve-sense system is the rodent. The tiny delicate form of the rodent, with unspecialized limbs (five-fingered form), a digestive system needing highly nourishing food, and high dependence on the environment, houses a soul that lives in constant fright and dies willingly. The rodent is always "beside itself," exhausted by the extreme activity of the nerve-sense system. Rodents crawl over the skin of the earth—earth's own sensory system—and so we see how the specialized nature of the animal is supported by an equally specific environment.

At the other pole, animals dominated by the metabolic-limb system fill out large forms by eating nearly indigestible foods (cellulose). Highly specialized limbs pound the earth, exhibiting the powerful will forces that live within them. A cow is a beautiful example of an animal dominated by metabolism. Deeply involved with her own inner processes, she is never fully awake. Earth gives her freely all that she needs, and her own body is her environment. She has no need for a nest of any kind. Calm permeates her deep, dreamy gaze.

The gravitational center of the animal is inversely related to its dominant center, so in nerve-sense oriented animals we find that the posterior end of the body is accentuated, while in metabolically oriented animals it is the anterior part. That is why cows (metabolic animals) have horns while squirrels (nerve-sense animals) have bushy tails. In the middle groups, these polarities are reconciled, and we find balanced forms.

The middle, or rhythmic, groups of animals, therefore, find themselves in between or pulsating. Their size is in between the other two groups, and their coloring frequently shows alternating patterns. They neither break down nor build up in excess, and the food they require must be closest to their own makeup. Their relationship with life and death is an active one, and they are always equally prepared to live or die. Clearly, these animals are the carnivores, and dogs belong to this group.

Due to the manifold interplay of the three systems, a number of different animal groups will be found in each of the primary groups, exhibiting secondary, tertiary, and so on, influences. To see how much difference a secondary influence can make, let's compare felines and canines.

Both felines and canines are carnivores, but they hunt in different ways. Felines hunt with their senses—they prowl, wait motionless when they sense their prey, and then pounce with great speed. If the prey escapes it will not be chased for a long time, because felines avoid great exertion.

Canines, on the other hand, hunt by pursuit. Their limbs are made for running, and they will drive the prey until it surrenders from exhaustion. Running activates their metabolism. Canines tend to eat more bones, while felines need blood-rich organs and are exclusively carnivores. If forced to eat vegetation, canines can handle it better than felines.

Many dogs frequent berry bushes and fruit trees, eating fallen fruit, while you will never find a cat doing so. The reason a carnivore would eat plant matter is not for its carbohydrate content, but for the water and specific nutrient content (trace minerals, vitamins). An animal in need of healing will instinctively consume herbs. Neither canines nor felines have enzymes in their saliva to digest carbohydrates, nor any flat teeth that would allow for maceration of plant matter.

Canines don't mind being in water, which is connected with the metabolism, while felines prefer climbing trees, the lungs of the earth. If we observe their forms, we find that the posterior end is accentuated in felines, which makes them better jumpers and climbers, while it is the anterior end that is slightly accentuated in canines, with the front end heavier than the hind end and the muzzle extended (compared to the feline's round face). Canines have a pack instinct, while felines do not. Therefore, canines are secondarily dominated by the metabolic-limb system, and felines by the nerve-sense system.

The natural world, in its entirety, shows the balance of the threefold processes that exist in a single human being.

Just as particular species show dominance of one process over the others, so do the inner processes and organ systems of humans. It follows that there are corresponding functions in the inner and outer world, a resonance between an inner organ function and the species that appeared as a mirror of that function.

Let's take a closer look at the rhythmic processes of humans to see how they resonate with carnivores, specifically dogs. Will dynamic physiology confirm the special relationship between humans and their best friend?

The rhythmic system of humans contains two major organs, the lungs and the heart. It has to be two, of course, because the rhythmic system is the culmination of the polarity of two major systems:

- the nerve-sense system with its qualities of being awake, symmetrical, open to the outside world

- the metabolic-limb system, which is unconscious, asymmetrical, and hidden.

The pulsation of the rhythmic system is revealed in both time and space, as both the lungs and the heart metamorphose several times during embryonic development, becoming symmetrical and asymmetrical in succession. When fully developed, the lungs are bilaterally symmetrical, in contact with the outside world through air exchange and under partial influence of waking consciousness (we can willingly change the rate and amplitude of our breathing, up to a point). These qualities point to the secondary influence of the nerve-sense system in the formation of the lungs, resonant with the feline species.

The heart has no direct contact with the outside world. The left and right sides are separated by a plane that is twisted, and therefore not symmetrical. The left side has thicker muscles, which form a spiral, another spatial quality of the metabolic system. The apex of the heart is tipped toward the left and front, and the heart itself is seated more to the left. It is the metabolic system that exerts the secondary influence on the heart.

So, the human heart and the canine species are both formed through the primary influence of the rhythmic process and the secondary influence of the metabolism. That is why Dog is truly "man's best friend," and no other domestic species can take its place. A dog is not a convenient nor an emotional choice, but a resonant choice, physiologically closest to the human heart. But what about the fact that the same resonance exists for all canines? No one has ever said that Wolf is "man's best friend."

4

Love and Hate

The threefold organization showed us that the dynamic relationship between humans and canines is based in living biology and resonant with the human heart. Therefore, we should expect the canine species to embody the quality of the heart. Specifically I am referring to empathy being a reflection of the heart as a sense organ and an integrator of experience. Empathy is the ability to participate with another, to listen to voices other than one's own. What do canines reveal in this respect?

They have the capacity for empathy that crosses the species barrier, and are therefore capable of holding great emotional charge. The wolf hunts prey many times its size, and such hunting cannot depend on surprise, chance, speed, or strength. It actually depends on empathy. The wolf and its prey both engage in a sacred game of death, which is dependent on locking the eyes and having a "conversation."

Many field biologists and researchers have observed wolves move through a prey herd (whether bison, moose, or caribou), where the all animals remain undisturbed except one, which locks eyes with the wolves and runs. Its entire life has taught this animal to hold its ground in order to survive, and yet on that day it runs. The wolf has asked, and the prey has answered. Inevitably, when the researchers examined the remains, they found that the animal was diseased, injured, or weakened by parasites. A deep symbiotic relationship exists between wolves and their prey—they keep each other strong and alive.

Wolves cannot transfer this empathic relationship to a sphere outside the hunt, but dogs can. Dogs are capable of empathizing with humans, of holding eye contact and engaging with our emotional states, of understanding our gestures, of asking us for help. And what does the human feeling for the canine species reveal? Another manifestation of the heart connection is the strength and amplitude of feeling humans have toward canines. A polarity appears here—our love for dogs and our hatred for wolves—and nowhere has this been played out more dramatically than on the North American continent.

Humans have feared many wild animals, but they have hated only one, the wolf. This hate culminated in a murderous rage. It wasn't enough to simply exterminate these animals; they were tortured in the most hideous ways. Does that call into question the heart connection between wolves and humans? Not at all. I said that the connection is marked by the strength and amplitude of feeling, not the kind of feeling. And we know that hate is just distorted love, a consequence of a distorted mind. Two questions have to be asked here: What kind of people hate wolves? And why the North American continent? It may seem like this has nothing to do with dogs, but bear with me, it does.

5

The Continental Consciousness

The North American continent is a place of the greatest contrast in terms of the relationship of canines with humans—hate toward the wolf; love and appreciation for the dog. If we widen the picture, we see that the same people who hated wolves treated American Indians in pretty much the same way and with the same feelings. Just look at this Massachusetts law of 1638: "Whoever shall shoot off a gun on any unnecessary occasion, or at any game except an Indian or a wolf, shall forfeit 5 shillings for every shot."

White men raided wolf dens to destroy the pups and stole Indian children to send them to missionary schools. They gave wolves poison meat and Indians blankets infected with smallpox. They wrote of wolf scalps and of Indians who attack like a pack of wolves. Both were deliberately exterminated, and both were forced onto reservations. And how did American Indians view the wolf?

That wolves and Neolithic hunting people in North America resembled each other as predators was not the result of conscious imitation. It was convergent evolution, the most successful way for meat eaters to live. Conscious identification with the wolf, on the other hand, especially among Indians on the Great Plains, was a mystical experience based on a penetrating perception of the wolf's lifeway, its gestalt.

—Barry Lopez, *Of Wolves and Men*[10]

The above paragraph summarizes beautifully the participatory dream consciousness in which the American Indian lived and which found its outer resonance in the wolf. And how did American Indians relate to dogs? While the wolf was honored and celebrated in the ceremonial tent, the dog was unceremoniously kicked out of the ceremonial tent.

American Indians, like many traditional peoples, lived alongside dogs the way they lived alongside trees—without active interaction. But there is a missing ingredient in this soup, one that would have enabled them to resonate with dogs the way we do. So obviously it wasn't those living in dream consciousness who proclaimed the dog to be "man's best friend." On the other hand, there were white settlers who were disturbed by the sight of the wolf, but resonated with the dog. American Indians did not hate dogs—they simply could not see any use for them.

The uniqueness of the North American continent is in the face-to-face meeting of the waking and dream consciousness. The settlers brought with them the spark of individuality, which did not exist here before. The participatory wisdom of the dream state and its connection to nature was deeply buried under the armor of conquest. Upon meeting the dream consciousness in natives and wolves, a spark of recognition stirred within. Instead of recognizing it as memory and love, due to secondary coping drives, this stirring was perceived as hate.

It was the clashing of the waking and dream state that caused the pogrom of wolves in North America. That is why it could not have happened anywhere else to the degree it happened on this continent. The stories of animals in any land will always mirror the state and story of consciousness, so we can actually develop a geography of consciousness using the natural world as our guide.

The conscious effort to save the wolves today and the fact that they didn't disappear altogether is a sign that we still possess a remnant of the old consciousness, which gives us the ability to build a bridge to future conscious participation.

6

The Organizing Principle

If waking consciousness is the missing link that decides whether there is a resonance with the dog species, it means that the dog is not resonant with the dream state. Can we relate that to the established resonance with the heart? According to the threefold organization, the heart is the meeting place of conscious and unconscious—in our hearts we dream. But if we superimpose the fourfold organization, the heart stands out as the seat of the ontic organization— the "I AM." Full descent of the ontic organization creates individuality.

Now, the differences between wolves and dogs can be seen in a new light. The quality of the dream state is its unchanging wisdom, its completeness. And true to it, the wolf's unchanging form streams across the land in darkness and silence, like venous blood —the heart's feminine aspect. Like arterial blood, the dog bounds in the outer world, loud and visible, the counterpart to the heart's waking consciousness, resonant with the upper being and the male aspect.

Arterial and venous blood meet in the heart in the greatest quantities, but they do not mix. If they did, it would signify a sick heart. In the same way, dogs and wolves should not be mixed. In the creation of wolf/dog hybrids neither aspect can assert itself without harming the other, and both wolves and dogs become less than what they are. The creation of hybrids is a product of color blind, one-eyed observation that is unable to behold the unity in its diversity.

I will illustrate this problem with the story of two wolf-hybrids I have personally known. Their names and other details have been changed, but the story is true. Iris and Thor were bought by an experienced wolf-hybrid owner. Everything was done to ensure their domestication and proper human bonding. They were three weeks old when they came to their new home, they were extensively socialized, and frankly, they were some of the most polite dogs I have ever met. They had a large yet fenced space to roam in but were still indoor dogs as much as they wanted, and they frequented a dog park, never causing any problems whatsoever.

All seemed well until the day they somehow escaped their fenced area. Iris was nine years old, and Thor was five. Keep in mind that they had been living as dogs since the day they were born.

The owner had tried to catch them himself, but as soon as they saw him, they ran away. Is this dog behavior? What does a dog do when it sees its owner, after it has been away for a couple of days and its tummy is growling? Not run away, that's for sure.

At that point, their owner called for community help, and people came, some on foot, some on horseback, all with the idea to surround and catch the dogs. The owner himself said that the longer the dogs remained loose the wilder they would become. I no longer remember how many days they remained on the run. The people who wanted to help them couldn't find them, but some punks with trucks and guns did. These dogs died like so many of their brethren, in vain.

I am sure that Iris and Thor "the dogs" wanted to come home, but the wolves that emerged after a lifetime of suppression couldn't. They couldn't be changed, trained, or domesticated; all they could do was bide their time. My only wish is for people to understand that these animals could never truly be happy or whole. There is nothing a human can do to satisfy opposing urges of two different animals in one body.

Even though their dynamic resonance with the heart makes them similar, the differences between wolves and dogs point to different states of consciousness and different times that created them. The wolf and the dog represent a closed orgonome (sovereign bioenergetic organism), and behind the creation of each orgonome is an organizing idea.

The organizing idea behind a wolf pack is the hunt imbued with empathy. In accordance with the dream state and the deep connection with the surrounding world, the hunt has an unchanging sequence that the wolf fulfills. The perfection of the wolf's organization is marked by its unchanging form.

On the other hand, we have the dog, resonant with the aspect of human individuality. Individuality manifests itself through variety. Humans have held back their development to be able to create and immerse themselves in this variety. Their unspecialized hand can pick up many different kinds of tools. Then, here stands the dog, ever pliant, turning itself into many tools, fashioning itself to fit the human hand. Surely, some will say, it was humans who created the many breeds of dogs, but it would not be possible without the flexibility that was already there. The dog remains the only species in the world with such a malleable form.

So, what is the organizing spark of the dog species? It is work, but it is not work related to survival, such as hunting. Rather, the organizing spark is work related to emancipation from the environment and from the group. Dogs can help us herd thousands of sheep, find drugs in someone's suitcase, guard us in the wilderness, live with us when we are disabled.

Until the concept of independence and individuality entered human consciousness, there could not have been a dog in this world. It took time for this concept to filter through and become a conscious choice. During that time, we find dogs in their unspecialized form, as original village dogs, waiting. Dogs waited to help humans be free.

7

Two Kinds of Freedom

How do humans repay such a favor? Actually, humans and dogs set each other free. Freedom is a condition of holding tension right up to the moment when the built-up charge can be set free and experienced in all its glory. When humans apply resistance in terms of work and training, they set the dog free. We have all seen working dogs in action, and truly, there are no happier dogs in this world. Against the highest resistance, their drive flows uninhibited, giving them the greatest pleasure and setting them free.

It is a different kind of freedom that wolves need, and they tell us so with their form. A large brain capable of processing a staggering amount of sensory data, incredibly acute sense organs, a large muzzle and paws reaching out toward the environment—these all speak of wolves and their world being one organism. Only in their world, only when sinking their teeth into a large running animal with whom they have had the "death conversation" are they truly uninhibited, truly free.

People see wolves as being free to go where they please, but it is not so. Air currents and the stars, animals and the waters, the scents of the earth and of their family, all pull on them with invisible strings. And they obey.

So, that moment of discharge, at the height of the hunt when wolves merge with their prey and with their world, is their moment of freedom. The largest prey offer the greatest resistance against which they can discharge. To help wolves be free, humans need to leave the wolves' environment intact, to leave their world in peace.

This same recipe would be disastrous for dogs. Left to their own devices, the flowering variety of dog would wilt into unspecialized, unpurposed village dogs. Dogs need to live out their organizing idea of work in order to be free.

As our idea of human work is evolving from necessity toward independence and into pleasure, dogs follow right along. Many people today own dogs not because they must have them, but because they want to. If Rudolf Steiner's prerequisite for humanity's further development—that humans must stop working for money (in other words, that they need to work for pleasure)—is to be fulfilled, we know that dogs will be right there with us.

8

The Missing Link

So far, we have established that the dog resonates with waking consciousness—thinking—while the wolf resonates with dream consciousness—feeling. Since the heart is the integrator of thinking, feeling, and will, who or what resonates with this unconscious aspect of the heart? We can start by asking: when is the heart unconscious? The answer is—before it is formed, when there is rhythm but not yet form. Since we asked the question "when," it is obvious that the missing link in our discussion of the origin of the dog is the quality of time.

In the early stage of an embryo, when blood first begins to stream, it flows from the periphery toward the center, comes to a complete stop and turns around to flow back. This is the birth of rhythm and the gesture out of which the heart will form. Since every inner process and every fold in time has a resonant being in the outer world, there must exist an animal that is a manifestation of rhythm. What qualities should such an animal embody?

Since there is no heart and no lungs at this stage, this animal would be a carnivore because there is rhythm, but it would not be a specialized canine or feline. It would actually be a prototype for both. The primary rhythmic quality would be very clear, but no secondary process would dominate. The time of no form is the reign of the warmth organism, so we should expect to find our mystery animal in a warm place. Since we are speaking of the origin, as in the origin of the heart, the ideal place would be the cradle of humanity—Africa.

Certainly, the lion fulfills all of these requirements. Let's see how its form speaks. The lion is a pure carnivore, and therefore primarily dominated by the rhythmic system. When we try to discern the secondary dominance, we run into trouble. The lion looks mostly like a feline in its nerve-sense features, but lives in a group; doesn't mind swimming; and does not climb—metabolic-limb features, typical of canines. The front end of the body is emphasized with a mane (metabolic-limb feature), but the tuft at the end of the tail (nerve-sense feature) puts the lion in balance.

There is a great difference between the male and female that no other cat displays; in fact, most cats are almost impossible to tell apart in terms of gender. In this respect, the lion is more like an ungulate (metabolic-limb-dominated animal). And just like an ungulate, the male of the species is highly unpredictable. When a wildcat trainer falls down, the only animal he or she really worries about is the male lion. Yet the lion is also very much a feline, with those retractable claws (nerve-sense system feature). And so, we go back and forth and establish not a secondary dominance, but a rhythm!

By bringing in the quality of time—and we have to do this because the heart is the organ of the turning point in time—a full picture of the dog's origin and function emerges.

In the first meeting of polarities, when rhythm emerges, so does the lion in the outer world. With the differentiated heart and lungs, canines and felines fill the world. The threefold dreaming heart births empathy in the form of the wolf. The fourfold organization's descending "I AM" emerges in that space between the systole and the diastole, mirrored in the dog.

Procreation cannot be the origin of any species. Animals are formed space and formed time, resonant with the inner processes of humanity, each a complete evolutionary form. In summary, the dog originates in the waking aspect of the human heart, fulfilling the function of work in freedom.

9

The Future

Everything that was said so far reflects the present moment and how it came to be. Where do humans, dogs, and the relationship between them, go from here? What are the signs of these times that point to the future? We have seen dogs evolve from original village dogs toward multiple functional forms (breeds) in response to changing human consciousness and increasing individuality. We have seen how the organizing idea of work has shaped both the human inner world and outer world, as reflected in the dog.

The world of functional breeds is changing. Degeneration is rampant. Look at a certain breed and compare it to the way it was just a few decades ago. It can no longer be trusted that a dog will behave according to expectations based on its breed. The standard of form cannot support the health of an individual dog—think of aggressive golden retrievers, German shepherds seeming to walk on their hocks, and English bulldogs unable to give birth or even breathe naturally. Certainly, poor quality food, vaccines, and poor breeding practices have all contributed greatly to this problem. But what is the bigger picture? What is flourishing?

We now have so-called designer breeds, and mutts no longer look uniform. A visit to a dog shelter will reveal an astounding number of unique-looking dogs. It's almost as if every dog is a breed unto itself. Is that not a reflection of a separation from blood ties and the unique unlimited purpose of each human?

The functional breeds as they exist today are losing their purpose because the work that originated them is exiting the stage as well. Maintaining them through breeders focused on form can only retain the process for so long—the form is dissolving right in their hands.

What is truly flourishing is the number of pet dogs compared to the working dogs of old times. Maybe it is that work itself requires a broader definition than most of us assign to it when it comes to dogs. Here is my interpretation: Work is a state of tension/charge in which a dog is placed in response to a human's command. It means a dog is blanketed by a human's conscious awareness, as only an awake consciousness can attain a state of command. So, does it matter what the command is, whether the work required is physical in nature or otherwise? I think not! What matters is the state of mind the command comes from. Which commands exist in your house? "Stay off the furniture. Stay on the furniture. Walk with me. Be nice at mealtimes. Play. Sit by me. Be my pillow. Let me be yours. The kitchen is off limits. This is your chair. No, not that one…. No, that's a counter." Can you see it?

Every intent toward your dog can become a command, which places the dog in the state of tension, which is work and which makes both of you happy. How do these simple commands put a dog in the state of tension? Because the dog then must resist other choices, must "hold the charge." This is not to say that physical exercise is not important—please do not misunderstand—but you do not need to move to the country and buy a herd of sheep to make your dog happy. In fact, sacrificing oneself to make a dog happy is a contradiction in terms. Since the dog is resonant with the human heart, how can a dog possibly be happy without a happy owner?

Dogs are here to fulfill the needs of people, which fulfill them in turn, and therefore their contentment depends on our making sure that their destiny is accomplished. And the only way for it to be accomplished is if we are in the state of command. What exactly is that state? If you have seen Cesar Millan take the leash from an owner, and the dog at the other end of that leash changes instantly, then you know what the state of command looks like. Cesar calls it a "calm and assertive state," and the Scripture calls it "dominion."

And God said, Let us make man in our image, after our likeness. And let them have dominion over the fish of the sea, and over the fowl of the air, and over the cattle, and over all the earth, and over every creeping thing that creepeth upon the earth.

—Genesis 1:26

There is perhaps no passage that has been more misunderstood than the above. It has been taken to mean domination, indiscriminate usage, or license for cruelty and irresponsibility. It is none of those things. In principle, command and dominion, calm assertiveness, are one and the same—the state of mind that can walk into a lion's den and not be harmed. It the certainty of a physician administering a curative remedy. is the purity of an ethical intent, the compassion of Jesus raising Lazarus. The difference is only in form and degree.

Cesar Millan always asks the dog owners what it is that the wish to accomplish. It is a given that accomplishment is there for the asking, and that the owners are not constricted by perceived limitations in their dogs.

Any dog training that caters to the dog while placing limits on the owner, doesn't take the owner into account. Or uses the wolf as a model (representing the wild nature the dog has already turned away from), inherently putting spikes in the wheel of the evolution of consciousness. This is not to say that there is no value in dog training; indeed, every dog needs some. The question to be asked is whether it is taking us forward or backward, whether it is placing limitations or removing them, and which organizing idea it comes from.

If humans are to have dominion over all the earth, what happens to the wild species? What do we observe today that gives us hints of the world that is becoming? In other words, how will humanity's outer organism respond to the changing inner state?

The living world pulsates, and always has. Emanation and evolution dominate each other in succession. An existing paradigm emanates until it becomes obsolete and superimposed by an evolutionary thrust, and the new world is born—the unfolding source changes its form. There are cycles within cycles and thrusts within thrusts—evolution emanates, and emanation evolves.

At this time, the impulse of evolution predominates. We are living in a time of great change, with Archangel Michael in ascendancy. The emanation of the old astrality is ending, and the last remnants of dream consciousness are losing their hold on this world. The force of materialism would have us abuse dream consciousness and forfeit the right to cross into a waking participation, while the force of mysticism wants us to go backward and forget where we are headed. But there is a high road, and the signposts are already here.

Immediate reality looks grim for the wild world, with many species being decimated, growth rates plummeting, extinction looming. They are disappearing along with the native cultures that they were joined with in the dream consciousness. It truly seems that there is no redemption for any species that does not have a human-related purpose. What if we expand the picture beyond the material world? We sense the animal soul inhaling, building charge. While it is contracting on the physical plane, metamorphosis may be occurring on the astral plane.

An animal experiences self-awareness in the moment of death. We know that all experience is a treasure, and with the decimation of wild species, that means there are a lot of these specks of self-awareness being deposited somewhere within the animal soul.

Is this enough to bring out the new astrality? Are these species going to be able to transform, to let go of the old astrality, to mirror the rise of the consciousness soul, or will they exit the earth stage, not to return? I think that we are seeing the signs of an emergent evolution, subtle yet undeniable.

Many species that have been brought to the brink of extinction are making a comeback with the deliberate aid of humans, which includes interaction and handling. So are these species then truly wild? They have been stamped with the conscious intent of humans, which changes them. Never before in history has there been so much waking intent aimed at interaction with wild species. How many wildlife rehabilitators existed a hundred years ago? While humans certainly raised wild orphan animals, it has not been a conscious life purpose as it is today. Think of all the professions arising directly out of the desire to interact with wild animal species, such as specialized photographers, biologists, behaviorists, and others. Not so long ago the hunter was the only one!

What are the wild animals showing us? We are being bombarded by stories of inter-species communication and friendship. We see example after example of instinctual behavior being overridden, of animals acting quite opposite from what the survival instinct would dictate. (Think of dolphins coming to human aid.) The predator-prey relationship is losing its importance. Whereas once the only way animals could achieve a sacred unity was through the "death conversation," now we see the sprouting of the life impulse.

> The wolf also shall dwell with the lamb, and the leopard shall lie down with the kid; and the calf and the young lion and the fatling together; and a little child shall lead them.
> —Isaiah 11:6

> The wolf and the lamb shall feed together, and the lion shall eat straw like the bullock: and dust shall be the serpent's meat. They shall not hurt nor destroy in all my holy mountain, saith the Lord.
> —Isaiah 65:25

I am going to leave you with the prophetic words of Rudolf Steiner, speaking of the far-off future, yet existing right now in potential and in consciousness, full of promise of a world filled with the joy of animals:

> Darwin tries to explain the process of earthly evolution by the struggle for existence—but that is no explanation. The esotericist knows that the flora and fauna of Earth are shaped by forces issuing from Devachan. The more human

beings have advanced in their evolution, the more they can participate in this process. The influence of human beings upon the shaping of Nature is measured by the extent to which their consciousness has developed.... In future ages human beings will learn to mold all the kingdoms of Nature with the same consciousness with which today they can give shape to mineral substances. They will give form to living beings and take upon themselves the labors of the Gods. Thus will they transform the Earth into Devachan. [trans. revised]

— Rudolf Steiner, *An Esoteric Cosmology* [11]

Appendix

The Threefold Organization of Dog Breeds

I am placing this material in the appendix because it is a work in progress, and considering how many breeds there are, it will likely remain so. Nevertheless, it will illuminate the way we observe dogs and give a scientific basis for understanding, classifying, training, handling, and applying a particular regimen to different dog breeds. I also hope to provide understanding of how major life processes are influenced when we tinker with form. Learning the language of form enables us to grasp the character and the needs of dogs we meet, handle, or bring into our families.

The incredible variety of shapes and sizes within dog species allows us to apply knowledge of the threefold organization and classify dog groups in a way that makes sense. While every dog breed and every single dog fits somewhere in this matrix, I have not gone so far as to place them all. Rather, I am presenting a grid that can be filled out little by little and provide an interesting exercise for the holistic mind.

Keeping in mind that dogs are primarily influenced by the rhythmic system and secondarily by the metabolic-limb system, we can proceed from there and discover further influences shaping the many breeds.

Dogs influenced by the nerve-sense system would rely on their senses, have smaller or leaner bodies, and be likely to show color contrast with a light ventral and dark dorsal side. Their prey drive is triggered easily, but they are also easily distracted. The focus of their prey drive would likely be those animals who are themselves dominated by the nerve-sense processes. All these characteristics are found in the hunting group of dogs.

Dogs influenced by metabolism would have large bodies, a thick coat and uniform coloring. The hunting instinct is minimally present, and it is not easily triggered, especially not by small prey animals. The love of water is another sign of the metabolic influence. Since the reproductive capacity, which is dominated by the metabolism, gives rise to parenting, nurturing, and protective instincts, we should expect to find guarding and rescue dogs in this group.

The hunting and protective instincts meet in the middle, and they are found in perfect balance in herding breeds. Now we can set out the basic grid:

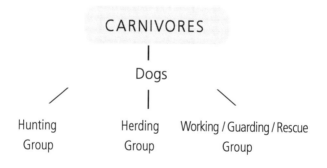

Let's take a closer look at the hunting group. The hunt itself has a specific sequence: Locate the prey, catch/kill the prey, bring it back to the den. Locating the prey is the part of the sequence that depends on the senses. The eye is the most conscious sense organ, while the nose is the most unconscious. Attacking the prey involves an active relationship with life/death and is the property of the middle system. Retrieving the prey is a giving gesture, metabolically dominated. Now we can further divide the hunting group: nerve-sense dominated groups will always be listed on the left side, and the metabolically dominated groups on the right side, with the middle groups in the center.

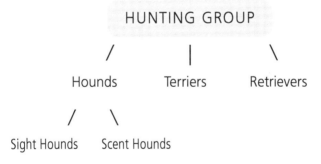

HUNTING GROUP

/ | \

Hounds   Terriers   Retrievers

/   \

Sight Hounds   Scent Hounds

Each of these groups can be divided further. For now, let's look at some breed examples. Whippets and greyhounds are examples of sight hounds. Slender, quick, and dependent on sight, they are nerve-sense dominated hounds. Scent hounds depend on their nose, the most metabolically dominated sense organ, but they still belong to the first sequence of the hunt, so we will not find a rich coat or a particular love of water among them. Behold beagles and bloodhounds as great examples. We can see that their coloring exhibits the basic nerve-sense pattern—dark on top, light on the bottom. The bloodhound would be the more metabolic of the two, with a large body, calm disposition, and less color contrast.

Terriers are a tenacious group, feisty and bold. They are all about catching and killing the prey, the middle sequence of the hunt, and so they occupy the middle position in the hunting group. Many have an alternating, patchy (rhythmic) color pattern, some woven so tightly that it forms the "salt and pepper" coloring.

Retrievers, as the most metabolically-oriented hunters, exhibit the love of water, uniform color, solid large bodies and friendly temperament. Think of the most popular of the retrievers, the Labrador and golden retrievers.

In the herding group, hunting and protective instincts come together. These dogs must have a high prey drive, but this drive is channeled into herding and protecting the herd and shepherd. They have to be ferocious enough to overcome a predator, yet gentle enough not to scare a newborn lamb. These opposing tendencies form a rhythm, so there is no wonder that these dogs belong to the middle group.

The conventional dog world offers no classification I could use, so I devised it in this way:

HERDING GROUP

/ | \

Focused Herders   Active Herders   Herd Tenders

Focused herders are the most sense-oriented herding dogs, such as border collies, Australian cattle dogs and Australian shepherds. All of these animals show "the eye," and it is not possible to teach them to herd until such time when they develop the focused stare (usually when they are about six months old). Breeders of working dogs (those who focus on function) guarantee that their pups will show "the eye." This focused stare is obviously sensory-dominated. These dogs are also the quickest movers of all the herding dogs.

The best representative of active herders is a German shepherd dog. According to its placement within the groups, this is the most central animal, so let's examine its form more closely. Here we should expect to find the greatest balance of the three systems. The German shepherd is a large dog (metabolic influence) showing typical nerve-sense system coloring (dark dorsal side and light ventral). With big ears and active, searching eyes, we would say that this breed is more sensory oriented, but then we notice a large chest and large paws which point to the metabolic-limb influence. Then, just to stay balanced, a beautiful, bushy tail completes the picture. It is no surprise therefore, that this most balanced dog of all is also the most versatile dog in human history, used for herding, police work, search, rescue, sports, among other things.

More metabolically-oriented dogs are those that tend or guard the herd as opposed to those that actively move it. They are the largest of all herding dogs, and we see a long and thick coat in many of them, uniform coloring, and a calmer disposition. Dogs that belong to this group are Kuvasz, Anatolian shepherd, and Shar mountain dog, among others.

And finally, we arrive at the metabolic-limb group of dogs. We have seen that the main focus of the nerve-sense group (hunters) is on the prey, while the main focus of the rhythmic group (herders) is on domestic animals. Now the main focus of this metabolic group is on humans. Here we find dogs that are mostly used for personal and property protection and rescue. Dobermans, Rottweilers and mastiffs make up the middle, very territorial subgroup. In fact, all middle groups are always more aggressive than groups on either side of them. The general theme of the nerve-sense group is flight, of the rhythmic group is fight, and of the metabolic-limb group is avoidance.

On the far right, the most metabolic dog of all is the Newfoundland. A large, fluffy dog, black or brown in color (like all metabolic animals—think bison, moose, etc.), with a greasy and waterproof coat, and feet that are webbed! Newfoundlands are the greatest swimmer, and, of course, used for water rescue. It is characteristic of animal groups dominated by the rhythmic system that their metabolically oriented members seek water. What the retriever represents for the hunting group, the Newfoundland represents for working dogs as a whole. The Newfoundland is one of the most patient and laid-back of dogs. The picture of this working group so far is this one:

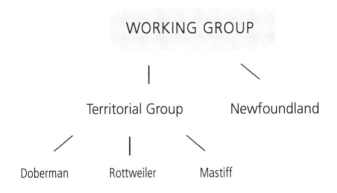

WORKING GROUP

Territorial Group   Newfoundland

Doberman   Rottweiler   Mastiff

The picture doesn't look complete, does it? It looks like we have the center and the right, but not the left. What kind of dog would we find on the left? It would have to be a dog with the quality opposite of the metabolic Newfoundland, so it would be limb dominated. These dogs would have to be fantastic runners. As they still represent the metabolic-limb group, they would have to be very hardy, with thick coats and resistant to cold. Since this whole group is human focused, they wouldn't be running after prey. There is a group of dogs that fits this description to the finest point, and they are the sled dogs. Now, the picture is complete:

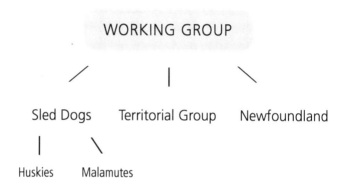

Since we are now more familiar with the language of form and are able to discern the interplay of living processes, we can actively apply that knowledge to shape the character and health of our dogs.

Each organism defines and strengthens itself best against the resistance of the outside world. Knowing the arrangement of the living processes within a breed or an individual dog, we can apply correct resistance.

Consequences of Ignorant Tampering with the Form

When out of balance, dogs that are dominated by the nerve-sense processes show nervousness, anxiety, hyper-activity, indigestion, shaking, neurological issues, and attention issues. The cure is rather simple: these dogs need to be made brave and sturdy. Their metabolic feature needs to be supported and strengthened in order to bring more balance.

We can see how these problems develop over time:

- Dogs are selected for breeding based on their looks and without making sure that they can still perform their original function. There is a reason these dogs need to be able to withstand the sound of a gunshot, as such training increases their ability to hold tension and steadies their nervous system.

- All dogs, when bred to be smaller for convenience for urban dwelling, or just out of fancy for that matter, tip the balance of the living systems and amplify the nerve-sense processes, making them more prone to neurological issues.

We can see plenty of evidence of these problems in hyperactive golden retrievers, paralytic German shepherds, trembling teacup poodles, and more. They don't tremble because they are cold, but because they are too small, and their nervous system is agitated beyond repair.

We discussed above the beautiful balance of the German shepherd, but that balance was destroyed through tampering with the form. Over time, German shepherds were made smaller, narrower, and with much lower hips. All these traits accentuate the nervous system, making it more susceptible to problems. That includes greater damage by vaccines, especially rabies, which is particularly deadly to the nerves.

All vaccines destroy the myelin sheath that wraps around and protects the nerves and the chromosomes, most likely through the action of aluminum, which seeks out phosphorus and destroys the phospholipid bonds that the myelin is made out of. Add to that insult the rabies virus, which then has a free passage to raw nerves. Is it a surprise that German shepherds were the first dogs to develop degenerative myelopathy—a progressive paralysis? Their spine already strained, not having any proper support, this is a dog that virtually walks on its hocks.

Over the long term, this can only be changed by taking such dogs out of the gene pool and making sure that only stable dogs procreate. With individual dogs, we can affect their diet and environment by making sure they eat nutritious, species-appropriate food (dogs are carnivores, not omnivores), by providing exercises that increase stamina (such as swimming), and training that increases their ability to withstand resistance—in other words, that increases their courage.

An out of balance metabolic-limb system creates lethargy, obesity, overgrowth issues (such as hip dysplasia), aloofness, lack of appetite, and more. There is a tendency to want to make large breeds even larger, mostly for visual impact, which has no connection to function. The formative forces become overtaxed, and the form begins to disintegrate.

Dogs are plastic and forgiving, allowing us to alter their form to a great degree, but we tend to forget that they have limits. Size that exceeds a dog's ability to function should not be acceptable. On an individual level, metabolically dominant dogs can be balanced by increasing their motivation and sensory processing. Changing their routine, putting them in competitive environments, using a lot of sensory stimulation, teaching them new tasks, all help settle the agitated metabolic forces down.

The rhythmic system is out of balance when the other two systems are not meeting harmoniously, not unlike a couple who, instead of gracefully dancing, bump into each other and step on each other's feet. The outward manifestation is increased aggression and unpredictability. All middle groups are at increased risk for such imbalance.

Like a fast river with sharp bends that overflows its bed, strongly rhythmic dogs need their flow rechanneled and made smooth. They need even rhythm, structured routine, and above all, a purpose. This is, of course, true for all dogs because they are all rhythmic creatures, but especially for those showing disturbance.

Changing the form of dogs with no understanding of how such change impacts their overall health and function is unforgivable. The consequences are on display for all to see. Accentuating any system beyond what is natural for the animal invites problems. Even without tampering with the form, we can see that the weakness almost always lies within the dominant system.

Let's look at examples of other domestic animals as further proof. Horses are metabolic-limb animals with greatly specialized limbs. What are the two major systems that succumb to disease processes in horses? The limb system and the digestive system! Most horses with problems are either limping or colicky, a direct consequence of a disturbance of their dominant system. The governing organization of the horse tells us that these animals must almost continuously move and graze except when they are sleeping. Without proper understanding of their form, we put them in stalls and feed them only twice a day, and then are surprised when their health starts failing.

Most ill cats are suffering either with respiratory or kidney issues. Cats are primarily influenced by the rhythmic system and secondarily by the nerve-sense system. They have a deep resonance with the lung and kidney systems. Again we see that dominance and weakness come in one package. The rise in the numbers of diabetic cats is of course a human doing. The more the animal is influenced by the nerve-sense system, the more sensitive it is, and the less able it is to cope with species-inappropriate food. How many owners respect the obligatory carnivorous nature of their cats?

Luckily for cats, our tampering with their form stops mostly at the level of fur. Horses are less lucky, as we have succeeded at making them smaller than dogs. What happens when the force of metabolism, which is meant to build up and fill a large form, ends up stuffed into a small package? There are disorders of metabolism and reproduction; miniature horses are known for diabetes, obesity, hyperlipidemia, colic, and dystocia.

Any fault that is induced into the breed tends to spread spatially to other breeds and temporally onto future generations. It's not unlike a computer virus. In addition, like a hole in a sweater that doesn't get mended, it tends to become greater over time.

For example, a minor neurological issue such as facial twitching or excessive friendliness (whining, clinginess) may go unnoticed by both the breeder and the puppy purchaser. In fact, it may be considered cute. When the next generation or the next useless vaccination brings on epilepsy, everyone tends to be surprised, and say that they didn't see it coming. Indeed they did, but hadn't enough knowledge to understand what they were seeing, what was an obvious weakness of the nerve-sense system just waiting to break down.

An example of metabolism taken too far is a Pekingese. At dog shows, breeds smaller than the peke are capable of walking to the end of the runway and back, but pekes only go halfway and back. They are too slow, they get too tired, their coat is too thick so they easily overheat, many births end up as C-sections, and many don't have any incisors (a cow feature). In the name of cuteness, we took the function out of the dog.

What the dog species needs is knowledgeable and responsible breeders who will breed function back into the dog, who will understand the indivisible relationship between function, form, and health of their dogs. The breeders of the future will need another faculty, that of curiosity and wonder. They must be able to ask the right questions, such as "What does a dog need to do and to be like?"

The capacity of creative imagination must now enter the dog breeding stage. In a way, the process has already begun with the creation of so-called designer breeds. However, that is a shallow aspect of a true process that will inevitably unfold as the evolutionary thrust sweeps across all aspects of our being.

As we have already discussed, maintaining the existing breeds with the ever-tightening gene pool and the loss of original purpose is going to be harder and harder. This is the end of one paradigm and the beginning of another—a time of extrasensorial creativity, inspiration, and imagination.

Notes

1. www.leecharleskelley.com/top10myths/dogsarenotpredators.html.

2. Coppinger, Raymond and Lorna. *Dogs: A Startling New Understanding of Canine Origin, Behavior and Evolution.* p. 61.

3. Charles Darwin, *On The Origin of Species.* p. 61.

4. Dr. Karl König, *Embryology and World Evolution.* p. 27.

5. Pierre Teilhard de Chardin, *The Phenomenon of Man.* p. 152.

6. Rudolf Steiner, *Foundations of Esotericism.* Berlin, September 26, 1905.

7. Goethe, *Conversations of Goethe with Johann Peter Eckermann*, p. 388.

8. Wolfgang Schad. *Man and Mammals: Toward a Biology of Form.* Preface, p. 4.

9. Rudolf Steiner, *Riddles of the Soul.*

10. Barry Lopez, *Of Wolves and Men.* p. 101.

11. Rudolf Steiner. *An Esoteric Cosmology*, Lecture XI: "The Devachanic World (Heaven)."

Bibliography and Resources

Barfield, Owen. *Saving the Appearances: A Study in Idolatry.* Wesleyan University Press 1988

Behan, Kevin. *Natural Dog Training.* NDT Press 2009

Bortoft, Henri. *The Wholeness of Nature: Goethe's Way Toward a Science of Conscious Participation in Nature.* Great Barrington, MA Lindisfarne Books 1996

Coppinger, Raymond and Lorna. *Dogs: A Startling New Understanding of Canine Origin, Behavior and Evolution.* Simon & Schuster 2001

Darwin, Charles. *On The Origin of Species.* Chapter III, "Struggle for Existence"

Goethe, Johann Wolfgang. *The Metamorphosis of Plants.* The MIT Press 2009

Goethe, Johann Wolfgang. *Conversations of Goethe with Johann Peter Eckermann.* De Capo Press 1998

König, Karl. *Embryology and World Evolution.* TWT Publications Ltd 2000

Lopez, Barry. *Of Wolves and Men.* p. 30. Simon & Schuster 2004

Price, Weston A. *Nutrition and Physical Degeneration.* Price Pottenger Nutrition 2008

Schad, Wolfgang. *Man and Mammals: Toward a Biology of Form.* Waldorf Press 1977

Steiner, Rudolf. *Foundations of Esotericism:* Lecture I, Berlin, September 26, 1905. Rudolf Steiner Press 1983

————. *Riddles of the Soul.* Chestnut Ridge, NY: Mercury Press

————. *An Esoteric Cosmology*, Lecture XI: "The Devachanic World (Heaven)." Great Barrington, MA: SteinerBooks 2008

Teilhard de Chardin, Pierre. *The Phenomenon of Man.* p. 152. New York: Harper & Row 1959

van der Bie, Guus and Machteld Huber, eds. *Foundations of Anthroposophical Medicine: A Training Manual.* Floris Books 2004